CONSERVATORY CANADA™

New Millennium Piano Series
PRE-GRADE 1

© 1999 Conservatory Canada
Published and Distributed by Novus Via Music Group Inc.
Edition updated May 2016
All Rights Reserved

ISBN 978-0-88909-210-5

Novus Via Music Group Inc.
189 Douglas Street, Stratford, Ontario, Canada N5A 5P8
(519) 273-7520   www.NVmusicgroup.com

cover design:
Robin E. Cook, AOCA

About the Series

The *New Millennium Piano Series* is the official repertoire books for CONSERVATORY CANADA™ examinations. This graded series, in eleven volumes (Pre-Grade 1 to Grade 10), is designed not only to serve the needs of teachers and students for examinations, but it is also a valuable teaching resource and comprehensive anthology for any pianist. The list pieces in grades 1 to 10 have been carefully selected and edited, and represent repertoire from the Baroque, Classical, Romantic/Impressionist, and 20th century periods. This Pre-Grade 1 volume is a collection of varied and delightful pieces to inspire young musicians and to develop musical skills. Many Canadian composers working in Canada are well represented in the series.

Table of Contents

Piano Solos

Piano Duets

*indicates Canadian composer

FUN ON THE FARM

Traditional
arr. F. Balodis

AUTUMN COLORS

from *Autumn Suite*

Beatrice A. Miller

Gently ♩ = 108-120

mp Au - tumn leaves are gent - ly fall - ing down, ___ co - lour - ing the

earth with reds and browns. ___ Then there are the yel - lows and the

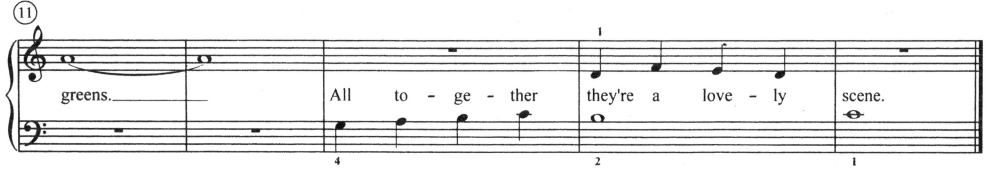

greens. ___ All to - ge - ther they're a love - ly scene.

County Fair

Christopher Norton

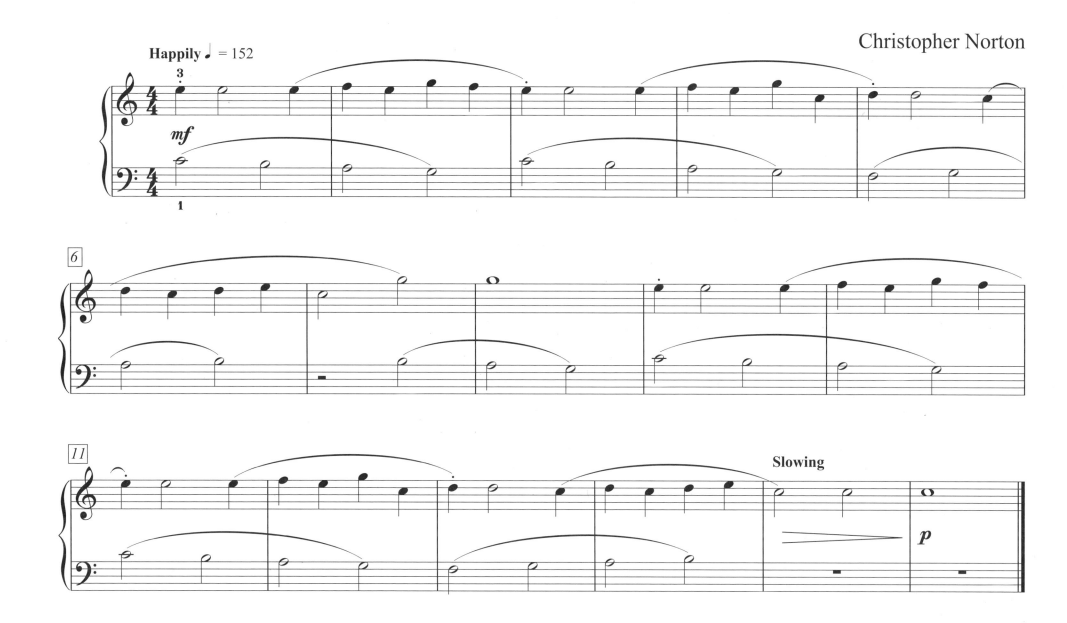

EASTER BUNNY'S CRADLE SONG

from *Our Animal Friends*

*Boris Berlin

Time To Begin

Sixty Pieces Crafted for Aspiring Pianists

Daniel Gottlob Türk

THE BEAUTIFUL BRIDE

Ukrainian folk song

Moderately ♩. = 66-80

Mikrokosmos

Volume 1: Six Unison Melodies, No. 3

Béla Bartók

After Beyer

Scott McBride Smith

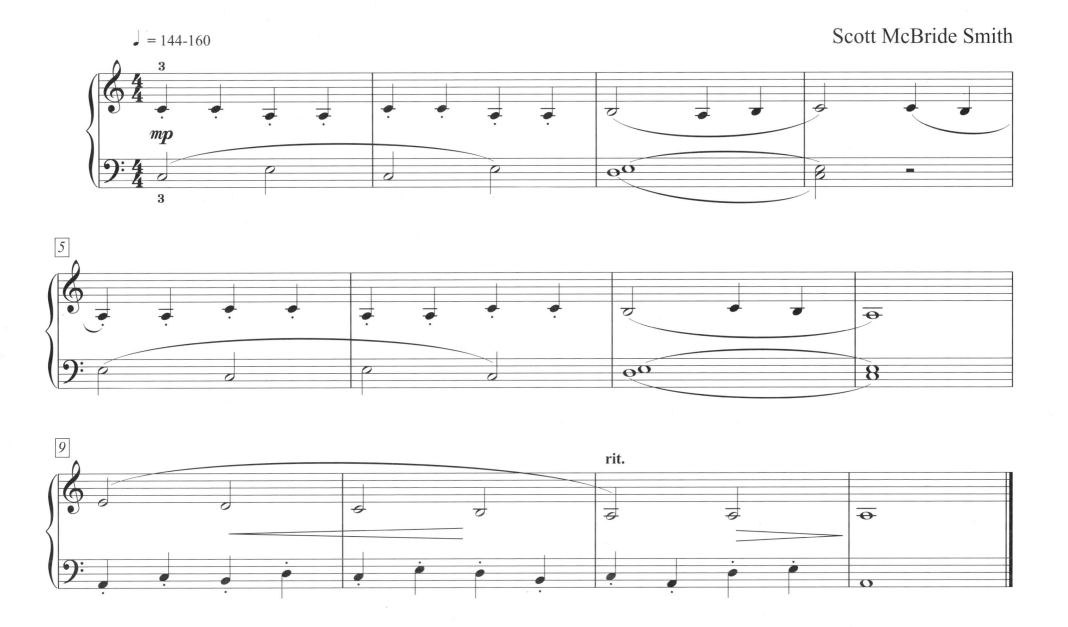

I'SE THE B'Y

*Newfoundland folk song
arr. D.F. Cook

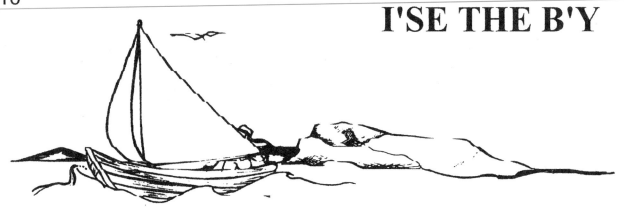

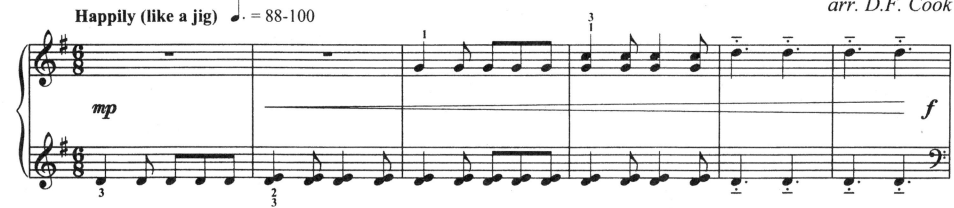

Happily (like a jig) ♩. = 88-100

vary your choice throughout the piece.

Used by permission of the arranger.

Play only black notes with both arms.
Use the pedal to sustain the sound.

Ebb And Flow

Christopher Norton

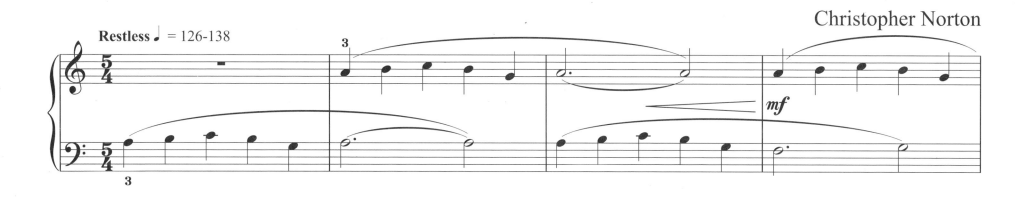

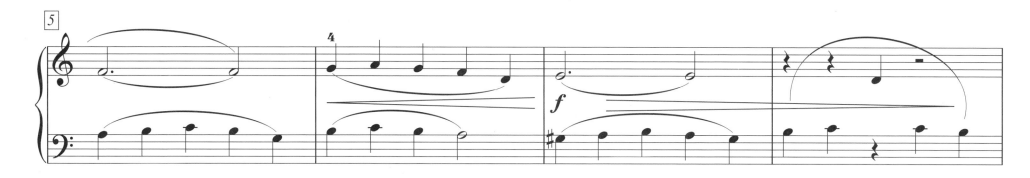

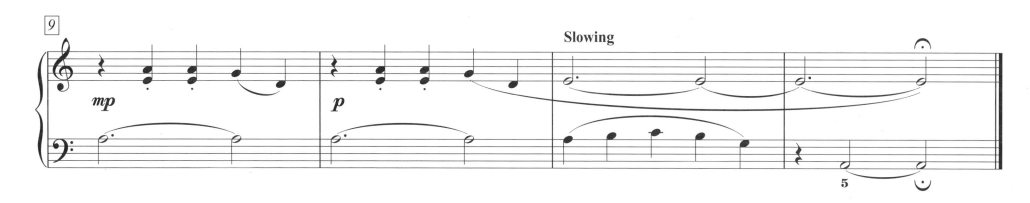

HAPPY BIRTHDAY

Mildred J. & Patty S. Hill
arr. D.F. Cook

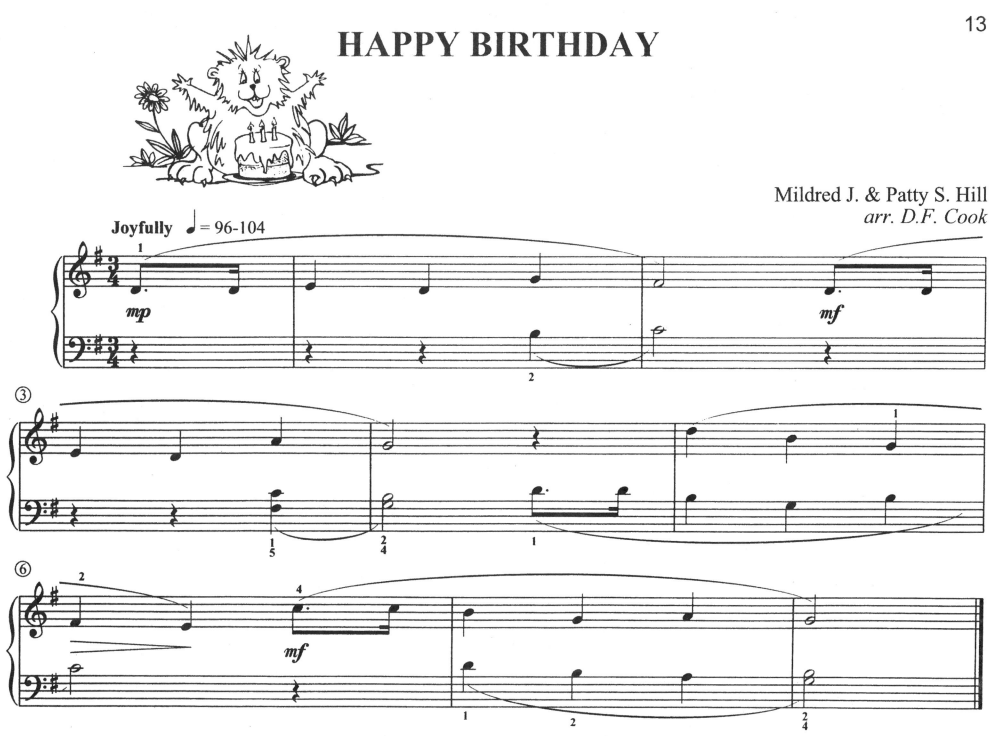

WITCHES WALTZ

from *Hallowe'en Treats*

*Debra Wanless

Irish Tune

Christopher Norton

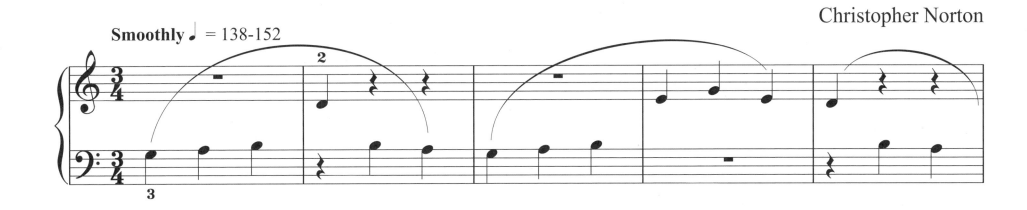

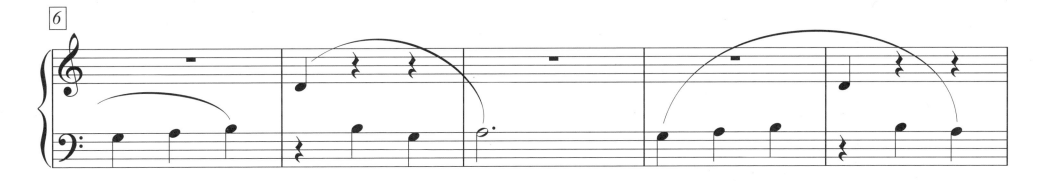

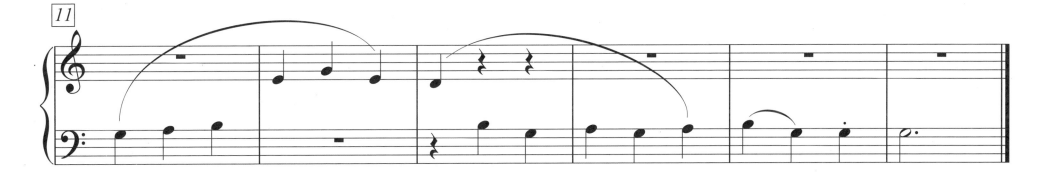

IN A CHINESE GARDEN

*Debra Wanless

hold both pedals throughout

* Glissando on black keys

BEAR'S LULLABY

from *A Bear's Journey Into Space*

Hanne Bramsen

Little Dance

Cornelius Gurlitt

Melody

Op. 218, No. 18

Louis Köhler

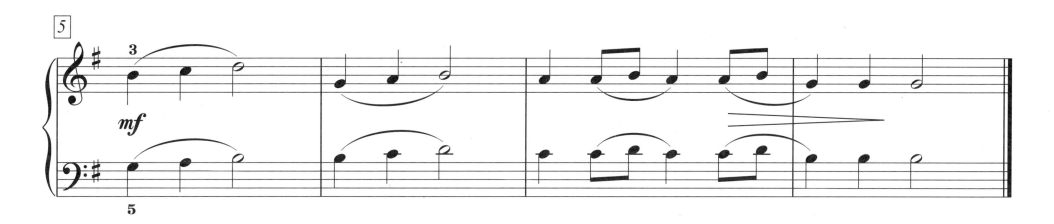

THREE WISE MONKEYS

Martha Mier

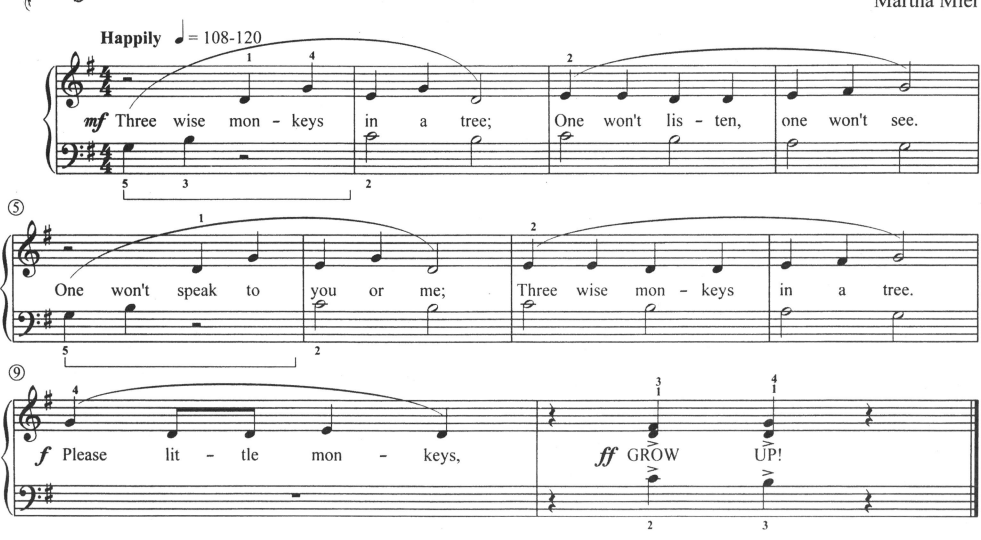

Three wise mon - keys in a tree; One won't lis - ten, one won't see.

One won't speak to you or me; Three wise mon - keys in a tree.

Please lit - tle mon - keys, GROW UP!

RELAYS

Alexander Tcherepnin

'TWAS IN THE MOON OF WINTERTIME
SECONDO

*Traditional Huron carol
arr. Benedict

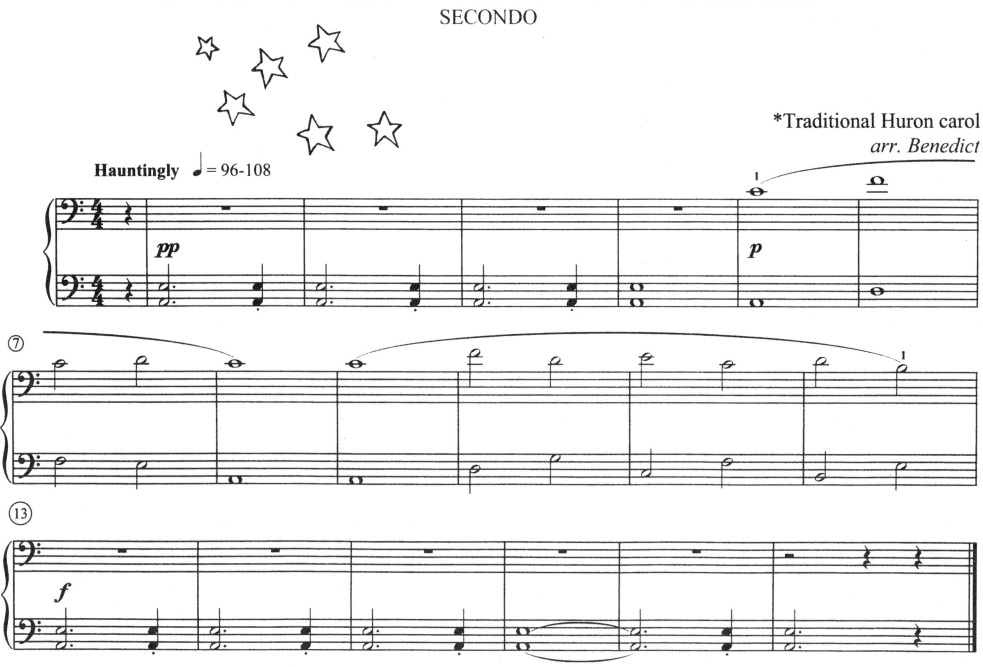

'TWAS IN THE MOON OF WINTERTIME

PRIMO

Play this page an octave higher than it is written.

Traditional Huron carol
arr. Benedict

Hauntingly ♩ = 96-108

'Twas in the moon of win-ter-time, when all the birds had fled, that migh ty Git-chi Man-i-tou sent

an – gel choirs in stead; be – fore their light the stars grew dim, and won – d'ring hun-ters heard the hymn:_

Je – sus your King is born, Je – sus is born, in ex – cel – sis glo – ri – a.

Source: Christmas Carols For Easy Piano

SMOKE SIGNALS
SECONDO

David Karp

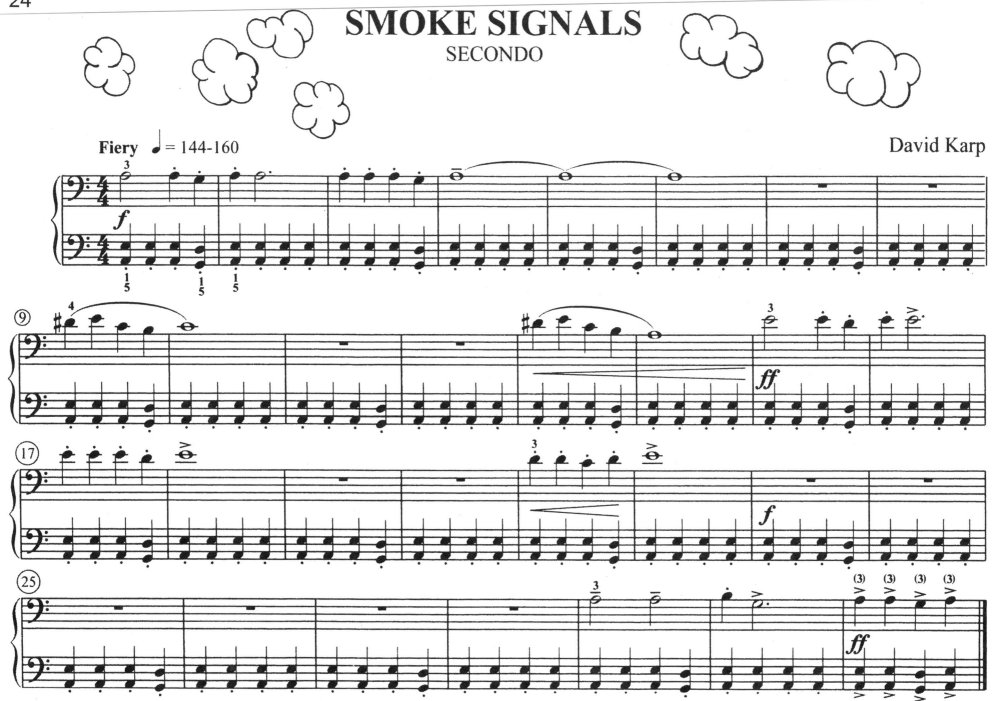

SMOKE SIGNALS
PRIMO

David Karp

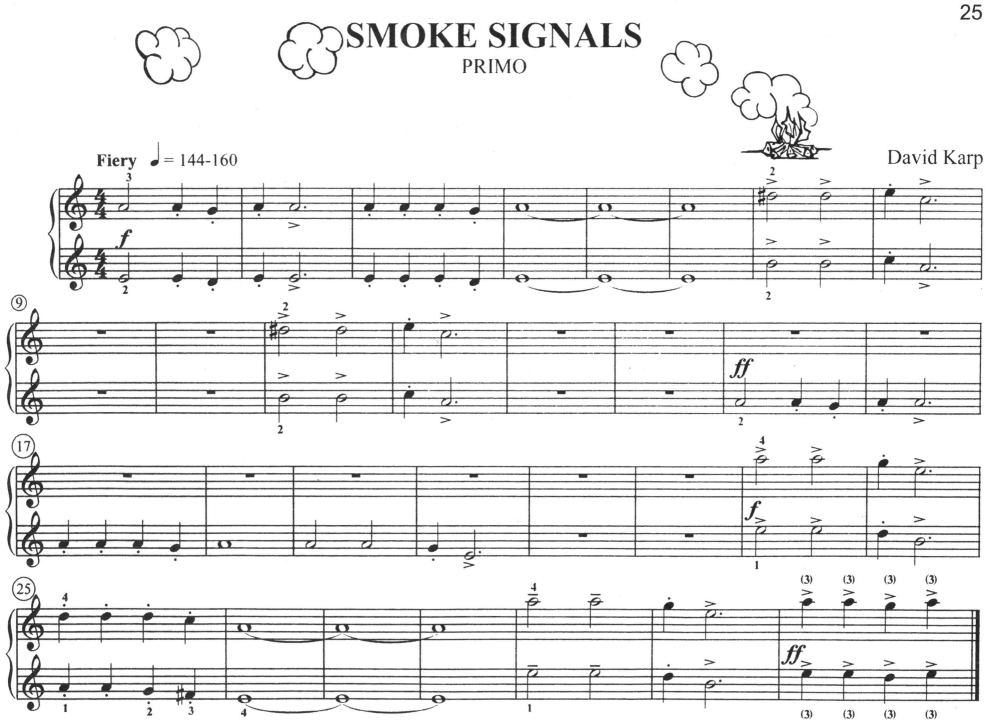

PUPPY LOVE

from *Duets for Dog Lovers*
SECONDO

Margaret Goldston

Play both hands an octave lower throughout.

Affectionately ♩ = 96-112

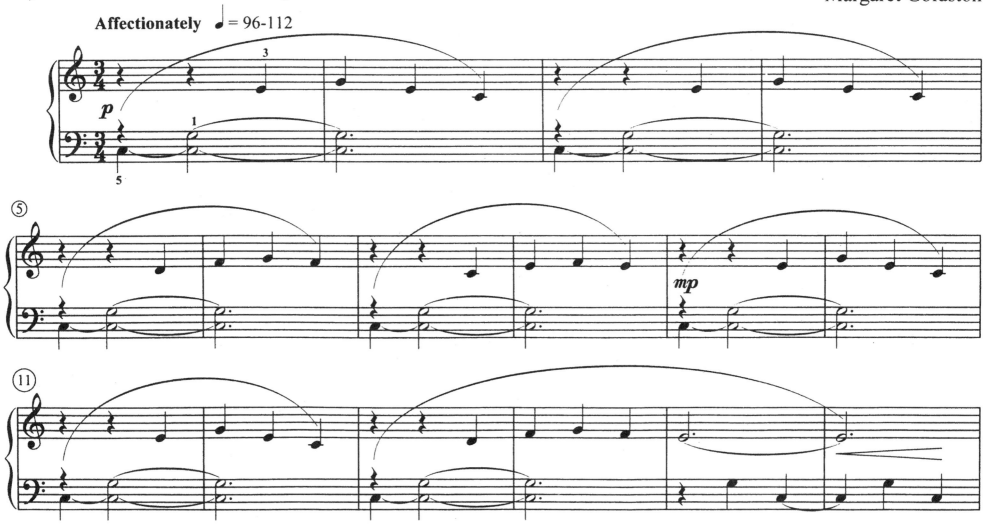

PUPPY LOVE

from *Duets for Dog Lovers*
PRIMO

Margaret Goldston

Play both hands an octave higher throughout.

PUPPY LOVE (SECONDO)

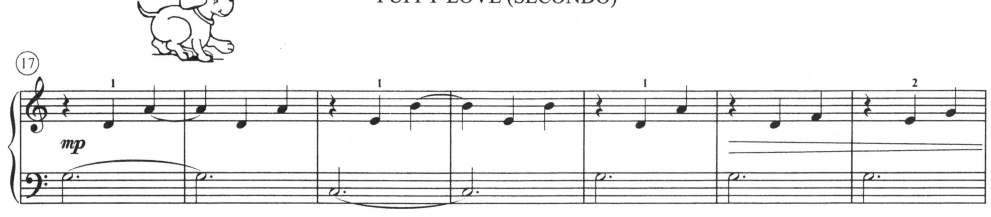

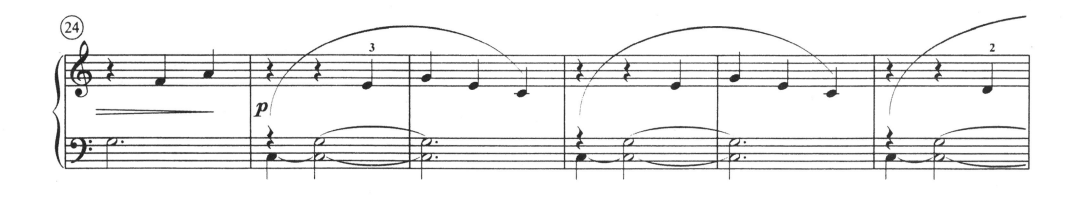

PUPPY LOVE (PRIMO)

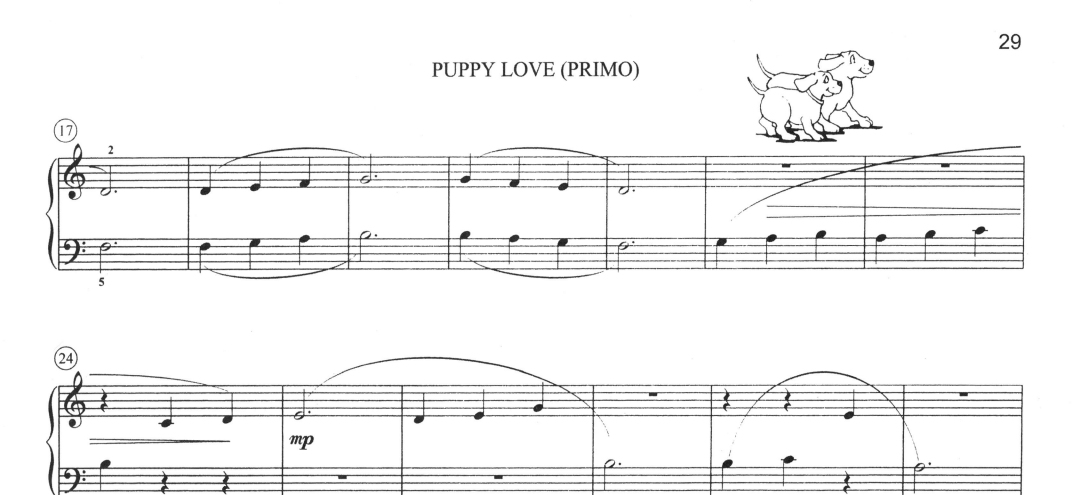

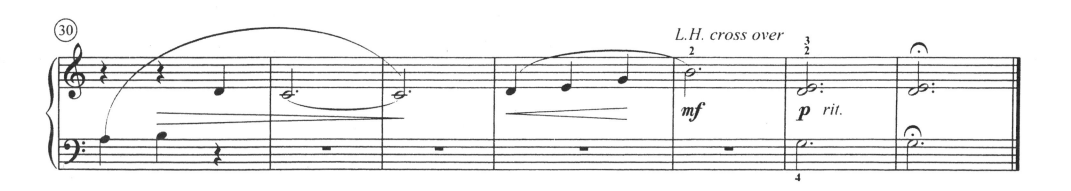

O CANADA

*Calixa Lavallée
arr. D.F. Cook